Mourning an Interior Country

poems by

Aaron Dargis

Finishing Line Press
Georgetown, Kentucky

Mourning an Interior Country

Copyright © 2019 by Aaron Dargis
ISBN 978-1-64662-063-0 First Edition
All rights reserved under International and Pan-American Copyright Conventions. No part of this book may be reproduced in any manner whatsoever without written permission from the publisher, except in the case of brief quotations embodied in critical articles and reviews.

Acknowledgments

Some of these poems have appeared in various forms in *Panoply, UpNorth Lit, catheXis northwest press*

Publisher: Leah Maines

Editor: Christen Kincaid

Cover Art: Evelyn Twitchell, *River Night* (oil on canvas, 2011)

Author Photo: Casey Dargis

Cover Design: Elizabeth Maines McCleavy

Printed in the USA on acid-free paper.
Order online: www.finishinglinepress.com

Author inquiries and mail orders:
Finishing Line Press
P. O. Box 1626
Georgetown, Kentucky 40324
U. S. A.

Table of Contents

The Garden, Ars Poetica 1
American Pastoral: A Sequence 2
Kitchen Sink 3
Mourning an Interior Country 4
Red-Winged Blackbird 5
Black Lake 6
Far End of the Lake Where Lily Pads Tangle 7
The Upper Peninsula, Keweenaw 8
Leaving, Mission Peninsula 9
Revisiting Sedlock 10
Map as Self Portrait 11
Painting Au Train 12
Grey Partridge 13
This Season, Last Season 14
Gather by, Myself 15
Winter Meditations in a Cabin 16
Walking the Field at Dawn, A Brace of Grouse
    Rise, Settle off to Heather 19
Along the Tree-line 21
Long, Quiet November Afternoon 22
Past, Speaking 23
Dirt Roads between Fields 24
Waking to November 25
After a Barn Fire 26
Calves in the Orchard 27
Southern State 28
Bevy 29
When Pheasant Hunting 30
Passing the Day 31
An Oak, Ars Poetica 32
Boundless 33
River Poem 34

The Garden, Ars Poetica

Let weeds be left to carry unfettered,
between stunted tomatoes, un-eared corn
wilting for water—

> the sun burns, dries, browns,
> with slight breeze, invasive florets lift.

I am indifferent to the dandelion tufts
floating—

> time is the dried petal carried to decay.
> My sojourn is seasonal mercy—
> swinging temperatures, ever changing.

I am left to the burden of bare hands
dry soil, no water. Weeds in the garden are not so—

> simple plants searching for life, green, green, life—

my ear is to the soil listening.

American Pastoral: A Sequence
American Elm, Ulmus Americana

We came here not knowing what else to do.
Cropped within the meadow a solitary elm; ulmus americana,
deciduous trees, pines, indistinguishable grasses
diminish into rolling hills.

Dry in our spirits driving the Divide
knowing nothing of past or present.
We pose against the softening
sun, mountains, *ulmus americana*, pine, grass.

We know enough of each other as distance from here to horizon
without asking ourselves about the weather,
beyond fault lines, leaving, not knowing
where to go, nor sense of where we want to be.

Is it enough on this sodden earth to acknowledge we share our lives?

Memory is meaningless without
where we are, where we are going. Lost within
our mutual disdain for the past, the unspoken—
not knowing what else to do or where to go.

We came here for the mountainous landscape, complete with
meadows, trees, grasses, flowers. We drove ourselves to this place
beneath the sun. Looking at it all, including this elm,
ulmus americana, our misunderstanding—

we are American, in love, without realizing.

Kitchen Sink

I haven't cleaned a pan in days
can't think of a reason to sweep the floor.

I've been sitting at the table, smoking,
watching a finch go to, fro her nest all morning.

I envy her task to knit a home, ever temporary,
lay an egg, hatch—needing a mother.

I press hard to my navel, feel each breath
rise with bird song, scent of peony

and strike a match to light
my last cigarette from the pack.

I picked the neighbor's peonies, arranged them
in a pitcher I use for lemonade.

I worry when he'll fiddle the doorknob—
liquored, speaking gently for my body.

I dream with wind to my back,
my joy beyond the windowpane

curve of distant hill. Another side of
idle life I lived serene in my ways.

The wind raises a branch laden with buds
bursting with morning sun.

Mourning an Interior Country

Waking is languor, first light begets an end of another day.
I drink instant coffee, bite of an egg, tasting of dirt
overwhelmed—

A trammeled creek parts
the fallowed sandstone meadow
abrupt mountains rise toward
grey-white clouds.

The distant curtain of rain is drawn against sun
patches. I belong to—
the void. I left, this morning,
recalling the scent of gardenia:
few of the good
left.

The present has broken my careless, ravenous ways
mourning the past, a shaking vast interior
all open: sky, flat green, brown, green land.

Tell me I'm stone drunk. I'll walk home,
constantly in arrears with the past.

I have a bed to sleep in
someone to lie beside.

> *Won't the troubles be towed along*
> *each landscape? no matter the beauty?*

I fiddle the door knob, shoulder into the kitchen.
She is awake, at the kitchen table, smoking.

Red-Winged Blackbird

September afternoons are cooling.
        Watching a blackbird with a red blotch sway on a branch
I recall they return to their birthplace to nest
        in sedges and rushes along ponds, lakes, ditches.
I want to believe the notion some—
        things return to their birthplace, not die as salmon.

.

Frost covers the lilac, paper birch yields leaves
        yellow, I look about to untended roses, gangling,
scattered stones circle around plants alive and gone.
        A red-winged blackbird stands on the frozen
birdbath, a tiny world in suspension.

.

November days are bitter cold. We stop along the road
        watch horses graze in the farmer's field.
A chestnut with white blotches muzzles
my cupped hands,
        trusting, I break   smile, the first in a long
time. I turn, a bird lifts from a post—a bit of red on its wing.
What gift, the drive home we talked.

.

The lake reflects the clear night—
you'd think we're of spring,
when mayflies rise and fall in a day.
        How many have I lost to inhibition?
I cast a stone, the sky ripples to shore—
a black silhouette crosses overhead without sound.

Black Lake
    An old photograph

Autumn, late afternoon sun angles into lens flare across
the boat launch, our backs against dry, hollow cattails.

The aluminum hull lights my face. The day's catch strung
mouths open wide in thirst, scales glisten.

I struggle and squint with false pride. Not knowing
my next return to this lake and those tangled reeds.

Now far from that wetland, I look across clay fields
and curved granite until blue.

I howl into hot day and watch
August burn leaves red, yellow, brown.

Far End of the Lake Where Lily Pads Tangle

I row into the lake's shadow
dive into lily pads—

      water forgive me. My lover patiently,
      waits ashore.

She wipes algae from my cold, brow.
I show her my past—

      blue lips and I'm asked to an idling car.

I leave the boat untethered to drift
open. We leave together

      for home, where it's warm
      and everything is clean.

Upper Peninsula, Keweenaw

Bloodshot from travel and counting change for liquor;
wind cuts wool and cotton to bone.
All streets at the harbor.

A redhead picks at ice in her drink,
glancing at rusted boats half-empty. She
laughs with ease at fear, loving the water.

I agree with her and abandon the meaning of wild.
I left her there nursing what is left of this place
back to life.

I refuse to accept this town has turned to stone.
Stove packed for the night—
dreamt I snagged a bramble, unable to escape.

I watch a boat pace out toward the horizon, knowing well
she'll return with something other than lost will—
as if gone out to watch a pebble sink.

I believe I've come here for a reason.
I'm not convinced. I take off my clothes and dive
into the lake.

Leaving, Mission Peninsula

We visited the farm house—

> clapboard painted flat white,
> green buds on cherry trees,
> blossoms open at any sunrise.

Talk is of soil condition, cherry yield, locations of morels—

> We eat greens topped with canned pears,
> cottage cheese and honey.

We drove along expansive clear water—

> ashamed of an industrial past
> limestone quarries and mill stacks

My paradise I once thought was, now
an abandoned light house
yearly, the community paints red.

Each overnight
I left my luggage in the trunk.
You unpacked wherever we stopped,
I wanted to linger
longer, awhile, by the road, but I didn't.

Revisiting Sedlock

The street name I remember well, the houses small.
    A blue house paled by weather;
    bitter winters, humid summers.

Neighbor'd stand by the door, smoke—
    single, mother, long dark hair,
    her young boy roaming.

She said a neighbor cut the dead tree down
    without explanation, gave me seeds,
    where to plant, told me not to wear gloves

        feel the soil?

The house is empty: sod laid, stump gone, tidy.
    I can't remember her name. Call her,
    Chippewa. Call her Sedlock.

Someone calls for a child. I look inside a window—

                By nightfall, I'm where I live now.

Map as Self Portrait

I'm learning to remember lost time—

Those lakes of the mind have dried, then filled
my reservoir of loss.

Rivers cut deep. I'm trying to find places
I haven't been. Where deeper into
interior country is now foreign—

    what leads the heart to such depths?

These maps have many variations;
misshaped lakes,
over/under estimated land
all mislead.

I don't want to keep repeating myself—
twice over. Gone is the word on my tongue.

Without a legend, I can't draw boundaries
of land and water—

    I continue to revise in my sleep.

Where on this sheet of paper will I recognize serenity?

I fear open water—
    loss, you can't control. This rock
    called past, tossed, settling to the bottom.

Painting Au Train

There is not a way to recreate the day.
Au Train brought me to a dream:

A grove of yellow brush, a quiet shift in the river
white papery birch stands
remove me from where I am—

>I pick a leaf
>keep, to return to.

Salmon have a sliver of a compass guiding
them home; spawn and filter off.

This geography of despair
has no limits—

>my leery soul, little sleep,
>>am I here?
>
>I want to know
>this journey out of the self, out of logic
>into nature, into pure emotion.

What is it they say about the past? The wind?

Grey Partridge

Livia, first empress of Rome, incubated
a single perdix perdix between her breasts—
24 days. I'm having mine roasted with chokecherries
and washing it down with a bottle of Viognier.

I'm waiting on a friend to phone from Charlevoix.
She went to the countryside to see the lavender farms,
cherries, cooled by the bay breeze.

She explained the scent of lavender from lake mist,
relentless wind, contrast of green, grey sky. Her lips
chapped and stinging. I think back, my memory, my past
becoming more like a tunnel—

frightening how narrow the other side is. I hold
the phone and am hit with scent of lavender,
damp moss, sap, ash.

I walk the reaped alfalfa field, perdix perdix hunker
until you've stepped upon a covey
only to cut against gust over the next bow to ground.

This Season, Last Season

Early morning birdsong
a budding iris
blooms then wilts within a day.

Less is left of winter,
       lost to the morning—

              I look back as if there were something
              misplaced after snow pack
              melts, drains
              mud-toiled streams
              natives call poison water.

Imagine kicking rocks down the street you grew up on.

I reach into the water to hold it back
for a moment,

       silt glides around my fingers—

       What will I make of anything
       if there is an answer
       lift me from bone soaked reverie?

                A bird chirp?

I place a stone where my hand was,
water parts. I stand,
       turn the way I came.

Gather by Myself

First frost, I watch a robin preen its feathers on a pine bough.
I slip back by the lakes—

>   the weather; warm, cool breeze.
>   All the windows are open.
>
>   Everything seems smaller—
>
>   looking to the ground
>   for stones. I turn, see water and am pulled
>   to soft lake shore, I drink—
>
>   a cold gust pushes me into the pines.
>
>   Its been a long time, everything's changed.
>   I am lost in it all, I recognize a lake, a road.
>
>   I cradle clumps of grass and stones
>   found. I drop it all in a field.

The robin stretches its wings, chirps, lifts from the bough.
The tap is running,
I gather my past spilled onto the floor
in no particular order. Day in, day out—

>   There is nothing.
>   I've remembered everything wrong.
>   They moved on, I return.

The bough is steadily swaying empty. Day has
begun I turn off the tap, resolving nothing—
between clouds and trees
autumn is stretching, struggling to a thin open.

Winter Meditations in a Cabin

> *"When I fall*
> *Let me fall without regret*
> *Like a leaf."* —Wendell Berry

I

It's difficult to tell when I last had
a chance to lie with
fallen leaves.

II

I awake from a dream. My father is rowing
an old boat around the lake. One oar
shorter than the other. I watched him pull desperately
at the water in circles. I call for him,
he keeps rowing.

III

I spent the afternoon watching clouds pass
out of existence. I envy their deliberate resolve
to move on, release what is inside of them.
I am here, looking.

IV

I picked leaves from the ground and followed
dried veins with my thumb. I placed each leaf
in the river. I drank a fifth of whiskey that day.

V

My unrequited love is wind.
I've spent a great deal of time
coming to terms with it.

VI

Alone for days in this Northern cabin,
I fired into a frozen pond.
The echo lasted for an eternity then,
dissipated to silence—

a crow drifted overhead with a single caw.

VII

I feel like a fish caught then released
gasping deeply for water. Once reoriented,
I settle into the dark blue water, not knowing
what had happened. I keep swimming.

VIII

The fruit of this field is without taste.
Clouds break the moon apart.
A fox is raiding the coop,
I sleep under flannel sheets in relative safety.

IX

Drunk on a single cloud
day. I can't remember my neighbor's name
In the distance, I hear a chainsaw running
cutting trees
down.

X

When I'm gone the land
I've tried to manage will fetter
back to an unknown landscape.
Weather will shape, sculpt, dry, burn
with time in no particular order.

Walking the Field at Dawn, A Brace of Grouse Rise, Settle off to Heather

The gun is not breeched, nor safety removed.

Watching, listening to the odd short call of brace
echoing against the wood:

'go back, go back, go back…'

An updraft stirs a few leaves,
reminds me
things cannot be undone.

I cannot abandon landscape,
near extinct flora/fauna
when will we
be done?

…

Grey clouds, hovered, filled days.

I light the stove, boil water,
percolate coffee.

Angles of sunlight
break on the floor daffodil yellow.

A chickadee chirps on a branch,
bounds for another.

The first time in weeks
I've seen the sun & sky blue.

….

Sunning in a chair beneath a tamarack
I look to sky
the day has begun. I have done nothing.

What can be promised of the day?

Along the Tree-line

I watch a doe emerge at the edge of the trees—
ear twitching thoughts to skirt into the meadow,
she turns and slips back.

Too much distance for her to have noticed me
slipping in and out of this world—
an open gap, my will against my own.

I will soon be gone from this spot, not as
quietly as the doe in this vast interior country.
I balk knowing it will be a cold night,

not ready to stand, leave this place
I've brought myself to. Return home
where its warm and a woman loves me.

I slowly piece myself together.
A dove steadily releases its waning coo,
I resolve to leave and brace for breath of air.

Long, Quiet November Afternoon

> *"if the wind means me*
> *I'm here*
> *Here"* —Roethke

I remember picking apples. A slight wind,
sweetened with blossom—

>   branches full, I didn't reach far
>   above ground. I bit in, field after field
>   glowing field.

I'm nerved by an open past, deprived
endless lakes, cresting waves
I cannot run aground—

>   my indolent time has passed.
>   I kiss stone and pray against arid south
>   wind I break my back against.

Scarce do I know the depth of anything;
lake, eastern divide. I climb out of bed
every morning, without uttering a word—

>   hoping for a small fire.

Past, Speaking

You're here now.

Standing beneath a single cloud.
        Isn't the past we ever had?

A stone settling to the bottom of a stream—

settle?   No, that is wishful thinking.

The sun is high. Flowers are in bloom.
I stand with an open hand reaching—is that you?

I've listened long enough to say goodbye.

My sigh is a song, played out
upon a tired landscape of rivers and poplars.

A cool wind against my back lifts my spirits.

I move along, toss a small stone
into the brook
watch it settle.

I dig my heels in   turn back and decide
to stay awhile.

Dirt Roads between Fields

Morning again. The day begins hungover.
Lust for a codeine euphoria is exhausting,
reeks of failure. The adage
'throw in the towel' or hat, something
spoken found in a ditch where
odd cattails grow without sign
of water. Thirsting for everything
green its all brown and yellow
in this killing mid-summer heat.

Piedmont grass is broke, bent.
The sky cracked, poured locust.
Rivers run biblically brown.
It went dark for a few minutes
an eclipse—
Bible thumpers left the streets
for fields and camps.

That warm feeling, a soft sun against shoulders—
clap, you're awake and not sure
of the time, nor where it went.
Cry loud, no one will come, try it.
Crest that grey-blue-green hill,
find the next town over, anything different.
No, keep moving, your car is new & gas is cheap.

Waking to November

I lie with guilt—

November morning light
Honey colored
filtered across the room.

Each unrequited sigh reaches for a last drink,
a last night, another morning.

I brew coffee. Watch a chickadee
bound around a red lantern turned bird feeder.

It hops to and fro
a task for sustenance
without need of thought—

>knowing
>what it must do to survive each day
>with nature against will.

I steadfast, by the window, entranced by leaves
falling one by one—

I fill the bird feeder, pick a pinecone—

>I kiss unconditionally,
>same a father would his child.

I give in to daylight and retreat
from the day, with drink in hand, light no longer honey,
and close my eyes.

After a Barn Fire

I smoke in the shower.
        Hungover, I can hear
each, beat,   of my heart.

Water drains with the day.
Isn't it, life, a sudden shatter of
glass
a bit of straw that ignites what we remember?

Shocking in a peaceful way.

And. I like you, continue on with
the morning, day, evening, night.

Continue on.

I smell char from an open window.

Beams black against tender sky—
light pink and blue horizon.

Calves in the Orchard

I pray each fettered cloud
to linger and form thunder
curtains of rain dissolve
this orchard.

No, only delusion and
more loss. I eat a blossom, serene—
thinking of the sweet smell
of your hair drenched in rain.

I stand at the edge of a row
tranced by the late afternoon shade—
remember talk of a child,
if we had a boy, a girl?

Southern State Poem

This state is in need of wind, certainty, money;
call it liquor. All public prayers are for full sun—
no rain, nor clouds, all go answered.

This mass of land, punished by an austere god
toughened clay, bitter peaches. Thick, ancient
tongues speak not Gaelic, but cryptic slang.

Humor is a racial slur. Mutter it, they all laugh.
No matter time of day, church steeples offer no reprieve
and have no shadows for people, animals to shade themselves.

That green wall of kudzu can't be slashed down,
it thrives on endless heat. Fools, return to
mills dreamed renewed, their children left home
cry upon deaf ears.

Daily, I try boarding a passing train, none stop
carry only cargo.
I curse the sun—
it bears blame.

It should be easy to leave, leaving, left,
but   don't bury me here.
A gust of wind will set me free.

Bevy

Frozen in degrees of verdigris,
I break at ice
for swans banked along the pond.

Gentle and seemingly fragile;
like a woman's wrist,
they dip their necks to tender hydrilla—

Wading in water cold enough to kill a man
before a chance to lite a fire.
Water beads and drips away like mercury.

...

Pre-dawn dusting of snow, delayed morning light.
Beside the shed, a splayed swan—
      hard as ice, blade of an axe.

The bevy departed. Snow and cold
masks the smell of blood,
lights the paw prints of a coyote.
...

Mother?
This life is short, the church doors have
closed.
What's ruined?
         What hasn't been destroyed?

...

The pond has thawed.
Cattails and reeds are now green,
lilies bloom white.

Wind and rain
swept everything
clean white like cotton, snow, feathers.

When Pheasant Hunting

Across the field, drowsing in the scent of dry grass
gentle afternoon heat weighs me down—

A brace breaks low—

      I cheek the gun, lead the draw, and pull.

A small god has returned to earth by my hand.
The echo of death is silent.

It's feathers mottled, spotted white and hazel
a green ring around its neck—

I've brought and returned nothing.

Dead bird, an empty casing,
scent of rust, gunpowder.

The sun against my back is no longer soothing,
I fire repeatedly at the sky.

Passing the Day

It's a dull spring day.
I gather morels along rotting ash;
      the standing, fallen, drooping bark—
      all possible vestiges.

I stop short a broken pine limb—
dried needles, drying sap marks time since
we moved south.

I'm okay with letting go of today—
      holding to yesterday.

My lover, wonders, prods

I drift with no explanation, responding
in terms of water—

      fluid, fills a shape, naturally forms itself
      or by man's hands, etcetera, avoiding an answer.

There is nothing worse than trying
to express what I cannot express,
but try. I can only try.

An Oak, Ars Poetica

Wayward in my ways,
now, I'm not sure my will
bends me back—

> an old oak sheds what it struggles
> to keep alive all summer. Repetition,
> steady silent change of seasons & moon phases.

I capitulate. I have nothing
for time to show. Stacks
molding books—

> tinder for the fire.

Why can't wind be grasped?
Try & hold—

> either a bucking horse
> or a dead fish.

Eventually everyone loses their grip.

What is displayed on the aisle of apples
is spoken for. Taken—

> what was given or stolen
> lies, a clear word, a vague one.

It depends who is dumping fertilizer into the pond.

Weeds too grow underwater.
A brush against the leg—
ever fleeting.

Boundless

> "how with this rage will beauty hold a plea,
> whose action is no stronger than a flower?
> —Shakespeare, Sonnet LXV

My bones take well to cold.

    Air my bones!

A radish pulled from the soil.
I am open,   I am dry.

A dust of snow felled over-
night.   Is a journey out of self
    begets the present,
    past and love.

Until the town you came from dies inside?

Could I bury myself in
liquor and return, pleading for home?
Before I could ask
    who uprooted me?
I sober and return.

Rage settles to a gentle breeze.
The clock rings the hour seven times over—
my silent pleas continue without reprieve.

The evening sun reflects fire orange
off balsam needles.

Distant rolling hills,   hold me.

River Poem

The river is un-dammed.
I hold to what I have—
   desire.

It oxbows downstream.
Tangled, I'm wasting energy
   grasping

uprooting ferns, dislodging stones
released
to current.

I've left all I have
to silt.

I'll settle upon a bank
of lush green moss—

      soft between my fingers,
      upon my face. I rest.

I fear the loss of freedom.
My body is,
weightless as a bird bone

in a hollow sky.
Where does the river drain
and mouth, open to sea?

I'm not prepared
to tributary out,
become landlocked in a basin.

An end, my end
is the splash upon
      boulder, stone, pebble,

at water's edge
      evaporating.

Aaron Dargis grew up in Michigan and currently resides in the foothills of South Carolina.

www.ingramcontent.com/pod-product-compliance
Lightning Source LLC
LaVergne TN
LVHW041602070426
835507LV00011B/1260